C000075960

Are There Really Plenty Of Fish In The Sea?

A Guide To Dating In The Reel World

Tony Demechees

AMP Publications

AMP Publications

For permission requests, write to the publisher at the address below:

AMP Publications

2409 Minnesota Ave

Norfolk, VA, 23513

Illustrations by DT Walsh

ISBN: 979-8-9904410-0-2 (Paperback)

ISBN: 979-8-9904410-1-9 (Ebook)

ISBN: 979-8-9904410-2-6 (Hardback)

Library of Congress Control Number: 2024906372

ARE THERE REALLY PLENTY OF FISH IN THE SEA?

Printed in The United States of America

1st edition 2024

10 9 8 7 6 5 4 3 2 1

For my children: Tre, Autumn, Malachi, Jayden, and Olivia.

Contents

Preface

Coming back to the ship after a long weekend, I sit down and shake my head, thinking how my time off was spent looking for "Ms. Right" again. I start spouting out stories of successes and failures to my fellow Sailors and how dating sucks. Then, as if on cue, someone says, "keep trying". There are plenty of fish in the sea". Most days, I would agree, but on this day, I asked, "are there really plenty of fish in the sea?" After that, I went on an hour freestyle tirade on how there are not always more fish in the sea. When that ended, I was approached by others who had heard about my tirade, and they wanted to listen to it. Well, after retailing my thoughts of fish in the sea, I was told I should put my thoughts on paper and write a book, and after many years, that's where I am today.

To give you a bit of background, my life's journey has taken me across the globe, allowing me to witness diverse cultures and accumulate a plethora of personal experiences. Much of my inspiration comes from my trial and error as well as candid conversations with people about the complexities of finding a life partner.

The genesis of this book lies in my attempt to refine my reflections into a clear context. What emerged is a perspective on relationships that defies easy categorization – is it a philosophy, self-help, or perhaps a unique lens through which to view the concept of a life partner?

While this book is undoubtedly filled with my opinions, it also draws heavily from facts and observations, creating a blend of personal insight and shared reflections.

Marriage, relationships, and human connections have always fascinated me. My aim is not to proclaim a universal truth or prescribe a one-size-fits-all solution to relationships. Instead, I hope to offer an alternative viewpoint on finding a mate, one that may resonate with readers from all walks of life.

This book is for both men and women, primarily seen through the lens of a male perspective.

The metaphorical structure of a day guides the narrative, symbolizing the stages of life: morning as early adulthood, afternoon as middle age, night time as the later years, and sleep as the end of life. Each chapter corresponds to a phase, offering guidelines based on age and experience.

Thank you for embarking on this journey with me. Now, let's dive into the chapters that follow.

Chapter 1

The Call of the Ocean

As individuals venture into the world, the pursuit of a life partner becomes a top desire. However, the challenge lies in the lack of adequate preparation to determine not only what is wanted but also what is truly needed.

For men, the journey unfolds against the backdrop of diverse backgrounds, economic statuses, and life experiences. Much of the knowledge comes from personal encounters, shared experiences, and conversations with peers. As young men set forth into the world of relationships around their early 20s, they metaphorically embark on a fishing expedition, seeking a suitable mate.

Picture this: a young man stands at the vast ocean, yearning to find a companion. However, he may lack the essential tools for the task—no boat, no proper rod, reel, or lure. In this context, fishing equipment represents elements such as the right job, car, attire, maturity, and know-how to attract the desired partner.

If the young man was lucky, he may have received knowledge from a father figure, such as where to fish, how to fish, and what one would need. Often, the absence of a father figure or a nurturing paternal influence leaves them unguided, unsure of the tactics required to navigate the dating waters effectively.

Undeterred, many young men venture forth with makeshift tools, perhaps no more than a simple stick or an outdated rod or reel. The bait or lures are uncertain, and access to resources may be limited, mirroring the metaphorical challenge of not having the right structure or guidance to pursue a meaningful connection.

In their pursuit, some may get lucky and catch a fish, even if it's not the most desirable catch. This initial success can lead to a mentality of abundance, with the belief that if one doesn't meet their expectations, there are plenty more options in the sea.

As males navigate this early stage, fishing almost instinctively, they often lack a clear understanding of their motives or a defined strategy. The surge of testosterone further complicates decision-making during this period. The initial approach may be impulsive, driven more by instinct than thoughtful consideration.

However, with time and experience, men begin to learn. Through trial and error, discussions with peers, or gaining perspectives from women, they refine their approach. At this point, a man may find out they like trout or a certain kind of woman. This could be superficial, like liking blondes or brunettes, short or tall, big or small. Now, there are different kinds of trout, and one may have to relocate to a lake or stream to get that rainbow trout, which could be a particular ethnicity or race.

At this stage of the day, immaturity and impatience play a big part as well. A man may be tempted to find places for easy fishing or the preverbal shooting fish in a barrel. When I was growing up, we would catch a fish called bluegill. They were fun to catch but didn't offer a lot of meat, and you would have to catch a lot of them to make a proper meal. It was quantity over quality, and even though it might seem, "well, I got that fish really easy," when they eat it, they realize it's not fulfilling and there is no meat. In other words, there may be no substance in that person or the relationship; it's superficial, and that person doesn't fulfill them.

It is during the midday of their metaphorical fishing journey that men begin to contemplate their preferences and refine their approach. The analogy of transitioning from indiscriminate fishing to considering a specific preference, like trout, captures the evolving nature of their understanding and quest for a meaningful connection. This learning curve typically spans the years from the early 20s to the late 30s, a period marked by increased education and a deeper understanding of personal preferences.

I made her laugh! She thought I was the funniest thing in the world, making me like her. I didn't have a car or a house, and money was not a factor for this short little Navy Seaman. The only bait I had was jokes. She was older and had more experience than I, but I cast my line and rusty hook, and I got her, or so I thought. I was so caught up with this fish that I didn't ask if she had another fisherman. The few things I knew at that point about finding a suitable mate was to find some-

one with a degree. My mom often taught me to ensure the person I brought home had a job and degree. It seemed straightforward enough to look for a fish, any fish with a cap and gown. What I needed to know was, what if that fish wasn't from the lake where you were raised; would that be a factor? What if this fish doesn't look like the other fish I brought home to show the family? Shouldn't I have a degree first? There were so many questions I wished I had the answers to but did not. I wish I could say there was a happy ending with the fish, but it wasn't. She was married and "with child," something I didn't find out until too late. I was stuck, and in love, with a fish, I could never have.

Chapter 2

Women's Fishing Expedition

Now, delving into the realm of women and their approach to fishing introduces a distinctive perspective. Drawing on both my personal experiences of being raised by women and having interviewed several women, it becomes evident that a woman's initial desires in a man are significantly influenced by her relationship with her father or the absence thereof. Scientific research, while not absolute, consistently suggests that the presence of a positive male role model early in a woman's life enhances her ability to select a suitable mate later on.

In the daytime of her life, a woman embarks on her fishing journey armed with a profound understanding of the kind of fish she seeks. Similar to the daytime male fisher, she lacks some fishing gear for the task, but often she starts with the essential tools. She navigates the waters of relationships with a clear vision, distinguishing between the qualities she desires and those she does not. Much like a seasoned angler, she interprets the signs, shapes, colors, and gills of the fish she's after. She selects her fishing grounds strategically, identifying the habitat where the prized catch is likely to be found. Similarly, in her quest for a life partner, she recognizes the importance of status, resources, and the attributes necessary for personal fulfillment.

This astute angler, aware that the big catch awaits, ensures she is equipped and demonstrates a commitment to the pursuit. Her preparation is meticulous, reflecting an understanding of the elements necessary for a successful fishing expedition. Just as in the world of fishing, where enthusiasts use specific lures to attract certain types of fish, she employs her own set of criteria to attract the partner she envisions. She may have a vision of how she looks when she meets "Mr. Right." She refuses to settle for anything less than extraordinary, showcasing a determination reminiscent of skilled anglers who meticulously select their fishing grounds.

Picture this: a young woman sits in her nice bass boat she saved for and heads out on a beautiful natural lake, determined to find a mate. She knows she wants a largemouth bass at trophy size measurements (or a man at a certain height). She may also want to make sure the fish is swimming alone and doesn't have any small fish tagging behind (or have kids from a prior relationship).

Frequently, the presence or absence of a father figure or a nurturing paternal influence leads them to the type of fish they want or don't want. Here, they may want to find a man who is handy like their dad was or loving as their grandfather was toward their grandmother. On the other hand, they may want a man that goes out and is social because their father was not, or rich because their father was poor and she saw her mother struggle.

Continuing our exploration of the fishing analogy in the context of relationships, we transition to a scenario where unexpected catches, much like non-game fish, may find their way onto one's line. In the realm of female experiences, there are instances where a man, not aligning with their predefined criteria, may be drawn to them. In these situations, despite the man's good intentions, a woman may decide to cut bait, metaphorically releasing that potential connection. This emphasizes that even with the best intentions, if a woman has set specific criteria for a partner, deviations may not be entertained, regardless of the qualities the man possesses.

The parallel between fishing for a specific type of fish and seeking a particular partner is evident. Occasionally, against all expectations, a woman may encounter an unexpected connection – akin to a different type of fish biting on an unconventional lure. Yet, the discerning angler, much like the discerning woman, remains steadfast in her pursuit of a match that aligns with her vision, refusing to compromise on her standards.

The analogy aligns with the morning phase of life for both men and women, where uncertainty and trial and error often characterize the search for a suitable partner. In this phase, individuals may not have a clear understanding of what they truly want, and their pursuits may be driven more by instinct than strategic decision-making.

As the fishing journey progresses, women, just like men, may find themselves dissatisfied with the outcomes. Seeking counsel becomes a common response, as they may be advised to explore different waters or change their approach. This adaptation can manifest in searching new locations or considering alternative bodies of water, symbolizing a shift in preferences or priorities.

Chapter 3

Afternoon Fishing - The Sweet Spot

E ntering the afternoon phase, typically occurring between the ages of 30 and 50. This phase brings a more measured and informed approach to fishing for a life partner. Armed with increased education and life experience, men now have a clearer understanding of their preferences. Similar to refining one's taste for a specific type of fish, men recognize nuances such as the type of water the fish comes from (was the fish caught in the wild or did they meet them by chance; was the fish found in a catch and release pond where the fish was caught and thrown back over and over again).

Picture this: a now more mature man sits in his boat; he may now have a fish finder or passed down map of where the fish are. He has talked to other people and now has a better understanding of the lures he needs and all the other gear that he neglected when he fished in the morning. He is more confident in his ability to catch the fish he is looking for.

DT Walsh

Factors like parenthood become significant considerations as responsible fathers seek partners who align with their values and can contribute positively to their actual or future children's lives. This phase marks a shift toward a more methodical and intentional approach to fishing, utilizing better equipment and a deeper understanding of the qualities sought in a life partner.

The individual has evolved beyond the instinct-driven pursuits of the morning and is now equipped with a refined understanding of personal preferences, contributing to a more successful and fulfilling fishing expedition.

As for women transitioning into the afternoon phase, a distinct two-part pattern emerges for females, drawing from my observations and experiences. Between the ages of 30 and 40, women often maintain a clear understanding of their preferences, much like the men in the afternoon phase. This crucial timeframe signifies a sweet spot where increased education and experience contribute to a well-defined plan in the pursuit of a life partner.

During the initial part of the afternoon, women, armed with their established plans, meticulously continue their search for the ideal fish. This phase is marked by a conscious effort to seek perfection—color, size, texture—all contributing to the pursuit of a partner deemed as close to a "prized fish" as possible. With resources, career stability, and a well-thought-out plan, women are strategically positioned to navigate various fishing grounds.

Yet, there's a pivotal aspect that diverges between men and women in this afternoon phase. Among all the equipment that a woman brings to her adventures is also a clock. Unlike a watch, it's in a fixed position, facing the woman whether or not she notices it. Unlike men, who can continue to reproduce well into their later years, women face a finite window for reproduction. For women, the biological clock can become a significant factor that can introduce a sense of urgency. The ticking biological clock becomes a constant companion, emphasizing the need for a more time-sensitive approach.

In the second part of the afternoon, as women approach 40, a shift occurs. The ticking clock becomes more pronounced, leading some to reconsider their stringent criteria.

The focus may shift from an emphasis on perfection to a more pragmatic evaluation. Scratches, imperfect fins, or external flaws may become more acceptable if the essential qualities are intact. They may say to themselves that maybe I don't need a "prized fish"

largemouth bass, but I still want a largemouth bass. The recognition that life is too short to adhere rigidly to initial standards opens up a broader scope for potential partners.

As the afternoon progresses and women near 40, their openness contrasts with the narrowing scope experienced by men in a similar timeframe. The metaphorical "night fishing" stage is introduced, representing a more challenging phase of the pursuit. Here, limited visibility mirrors the inherent challenges of finding a partner later in life. Luck plays a more significant role, and the approach may shift from a methodical search to a hopeful cast, accepting whatever comes.

During this sweet spot, a peak appears. It's not just the sun that is high, but women's sexual peak. Some women at this stage enjoy what my grandmother calls "footloose and fancy-free." They may decide to go sport fishing, where they catch fish for fun but have no intentions of keeping them. They may also notice that not only are fish their age biting at their hook, but younger and older fish are lurking around and nibbling. Some also call this the cougar stage, but one would be wise to see that it's a woman who has come into her own and maybe enjoying some much-needed confidence and validation of the great angler she is.

For men and women alike, the evening stage signifies a critical juncture. Whether they've found their ideal partner or not, this phase underscores the nuanced dynamics of searching for a life companion. The complexities of timing, social expectations, and personal goals converge in a narrative that resonates with the complications of human connection.

Chapter 4

Night Fishing - A Desperate Dash

As individuals progress into the later stages of their lives, the dynamics of the pursuit of a life partner undergo significant shifts, offering unique perspectives for both men and women.

For men, entering this phase entails a transformation influenced by a diminishing testosterone level and a profound evolution in mindset. The focus shifts from merely seeking a visually appealing partner to one where substance and compatibility take precedence. The man, having navigated the complexities of life, seeks a connection that goes beyond superficial attributes. Unlike the earlier pursuit of the "beautiful rainbow trout," he now values the maturity, satisfaction, and enduring qualities of the relationship. He seeks a partner with whom he can share a profound connection, akin to a fine catch that provides lasting fulfillment.

DT Walsh

He also has something with him now that seems out of place on his boat, and it's a distraction at best. He now has a rearview mirror. He looks into it and sees himself as a young man with a head full of hair and a straight pole to go fishing anytime he wants. He sees fish that he had, good and bad, and he may fight the urge to play the "what if game." Like, "what if" I kept that trout I had 15 years ago? Or "What if" I was younger now, the fish I would get?

On the other hand, women, particular-ly those who have not had children, find themselves at a juncture where biological factors could come into play. Things such as high-risk pregnancy become a factor, as well as cultural expectations, adding layers of complexity.

Women may open up to broader perspec-tives during this phase, reevaluating their criteria and allowing for more flexibility. However, societal expectations, financial considerations, and the desire for a family can induce panic, prompting some women to cast their lines in waters where success is seemingly guaranteed because "I have to get a fish."

"I have to get a fish," or I have to get a mate is not a notion only shared by women. Men have the same mindset when it comes to night fishing because it's harder to do. When fishing at night, you can't fish everywhere you would have done while during the day, or because now you are older and have more going on in your life, you may not be able to get around like you once did. You may need special gear to get the fish you are looking for or more money, more social access, etc.

As the day draws to a close, many individuals feel a strong urge not to return home empty-handed in terms of their pursuits or to face the prospect of loneliness, adding an extra layer of anxiety or resignation. In times of panic or societal pressure, individuals might opt for a catch that, while not ideal, ensures they do not go home empty-handed. The pressure to find a companion before metaphorically "sleeping" or "perishing" introduces an additional dimension of complexity into the process of decision-making. The analogy of 'Carp' fishing illustrates this point.

Carp, known for their bottom-feeding habits, represent a catch that might not align with one's culinary preferences. When I would go fishing with my dad and we had a bad day out at the lake and couldn't catch a thing, he would take us to this little reservoir to catch carp. We would put anything we had on the hooks, and because the water was low, we could see exactly where to aim to get a fish. Every time a carp would hit our hook we would have fun reeling them in, but we never took them home or ate them. I'm sure if we felt like that's all we could get to eat, we would have, but it would not be the same as a quality fish that would satisfy on different levels.

This phase in the pursuit of a life partner encapsulates the overarching theme of the book, where the primary goal is to avoid going home without the desired 'fish.' Whether it be the man seeking a profound connection or the woman navigating societal expectations, the metaphorical journey through the various stages of life underscores the intricacies and challenges inherent in the quest for a meaningful relationship.

Chapter 5

The One That Got Away

The imagery of the "big white whale" and the one that got away introduces a contemplative layer to the narrative. It highlights instances where the aspirations and efforts of individuals may fall short due to unpreparedness or immaturity. The symbolism of the fishing line serves as a metaphor for maturity, suggesting that, at times, individuals may not be ready to han-

dle the depth and weight of the relationships they aspire to be in.

One may come across this fish early in the
day and, with a little luck, may find this
fish on their hook, but due to inexperience,
the line breaks, and the fish gets away. This

molds one into how they learn to fish in the future; some learn from the ordeal and gather the perceived gear they may need to land their white whale. They mature mentally, physically, and so on, and they venture back to that spot where they lost their white whale, hoping to get a second chance.

I met her online. She was around ten years my senior, but you couldn't tell by looking at her. She was intelligent, funny, and sexy. Our chemistry was off the charts, but one day, she invited me over for dinner. I freaked out. I knew she had kids, and I was thinking, "this is it." She wants me to meet her kids. I was in my early 20s and was scared to death of meeting a love interest's kids. So, I made up an excuse at the last minute. Something like my friend stopped by unexpectedly. She didn't say anything right away, showing her maturity. The next day, she told me how disappointed she was and how she had made a meal, paid for a babysitter, and planned an awesome night for us. She told me she couldn't be with me anymore and that she was hurt. Looking back on it, I wish I had the maturity to voice my concerns instead of assuming things that were not there. Communication in relationships is critical; sometimes, you have to have hard conversations about fears and expectations.

Chapter 6

Trophy Fish and the Superficial Catch

The concept of the trophy fish parallels the social expectations associated with "trophy" spouses, emphasizing the importance of substance over mere external attraction. Instances arise where individuals acquire visually appealing yet ultimately unfulfilling "trophy fish," echoing the sentiment of having something beautiful to showcase but lacking sustenance.

A trophy fish has a general purpose of just being shown off. There is no fulfilling meal or support and nourishment provided by a trophy. It is there to be looked at and admired by others. No one ever asks how a trophy fish tastes; they ask how hard was it to catch and when will you catch another great-looking one.

This is not to say that one can't have an attractive spouse and be fulfilled, but rather, it's a cautionary tale of valuing the superficial over substance.

The excitement lies in the pursuit. Witnessing a seasoned angler wrestle with a hefty bass or a novice struggle against a formidable oceanic creature is both entertaining and enlightening. Yet, once the catch is made, it is often either released back into the water or preserved as a trophy for display. While it marks a momentary victory, it doesn't necessarily bring lasting fulfillment for the day or the lifetime. True maturity develops with time, accompanied by the wisdom that accompanies it. Relying solely on superficial appearances or fleeting thrills can only satisfy one to a certain extent.

I once had a friend who had a girlfriend and a wife on the side. He would tell us stories of his exploits with his girlfriend and would show us pictures as he bragged about how beautiful she was. I remember thinking, "You have a beautiful, educated woman with a career," and this girl works at a Dairy Queen. I can tell you that both relationships didn't last.

Another one of my friends liked the "bad boy" type. She loved the danger of his chosen occupation and fast-money lifestyle. Their love was fast and free until he got in trouble and had to go away for a long time. During that time she reflected on life and what was important for herself and her future family.

She realized that a mate is more than cheap thrills and fun times.

Reflections And Epilogue

In delving into the metaphorical journey of seeking a life partner, the exploration spans from the break of day to the tranquil night, each phase laden with unique options, perspectives, and challenges. This expedition commences with the dawn, characterized by a hopeful journey or meticulous plan. As life progresses, reaching the zenith of middle age imparts wisdom, patience, or compromise, eventually leading to the nocturnal realm where choices become critical, teetering between celebratory success and a frantic dash to secure a catch.

As we all get older and time passes, we hope to find the mate that was meant for us. Some of us are blessed enough to find them, but some go to bed hungry. You have the ability to gather the tools and supplies you need to get your mate. Communication, maturity, and yes, even luck will play a part in your journey. Are there really plenty of fish in the sea depends on you.

Glossary Of Fishing Terms

Angler: A person who fishes with a rod and line. In the context of relationships, its the person looking for a potential partner.

Bait: Substance used to attract and catch fish. In relationships, bait could be seen as the qualities or actions that draw someone's attention or interest.

Bodies of water: A specific area or location where fish may be present. In relationships, this could represent environments or situations conducive to meeting potential partners.

Catch and Release: A fishing practice where caught fish are released back into the water. In relationships, this could relate to the idea of briefly experiencing a connection without a long-term commitment.

Casting: The act of throwing the fishing line and bait into the water. In relationships, casting could signify making efforts or taking actions to attract and connect with someone.

Fish Finder: A device used to locate fish underwater. In relationships, this might represent dating apps, social clubs, church, etc.

Hook: The sharp point at the end of a fishing line that catches the fish. In our analogy, the hook represents the captivating qualities or actions that make a potential partner stay.

Line: String or cord is used in fishing. In relationships, the line could be analogous to the connection or communication between partners.

Lures: Artificial bait is designed to attract and deceive fish. In the context of relationships, these could be considered as attractive qualities or actions that captivate a potential partner.

Non-Game Fish: Are any species not specifically categorized as a game, except those considered endangered. They typically have no commercial value because they aren't appetizing, often thanks to larger scales and more bones. In relationships, this could represent a not preferred mate.

Reels: The device is attached to a fishing rod for winding in the fishing line. In our context, reels symbolize the mechanisms or efforts employed to bring a potential partner closer.

Rods: Fishing rods are long, slender poles designed to catch fish. In our analogy, these represent the qualities and characteristics one brings to a relationship.

Acknowledgements

Thanks so much to all my beta readers for taking the time and making the effort to not just read my draft book, but send detailed comments and feedback. This book is far better thanks to you. Special thanks to my family, friends, and shipmates who inspired me to finish this project and continue to support me.

About The Author

Tony Demechees grew up in the city of Akron, Ohio. He enlisted in the Navy after high school and served for over 20 years, where he earned his Commission and served around the world. Drawing inspiration from personal experiences, cultural insights, and a dash of metaphorical story-telling, Tony Demechees shows his passion for exploring the complexities of human re-lationships and the journey to find a life partner. He has five children and lives in Norfolk, Virginia.

https://tonydemechees.com/

https://www.facebook.com/TonyDemech ees2

https://www.instagram.com/tonydemeche es/

https://www.goodreads.com/tonydemech ees